Level C Book 1

P9-DMU-883

Dr. Funster's
THINK-A-MINUTES

Fast, Fun Brainwork
for Higher Grades
and Top Test Scores

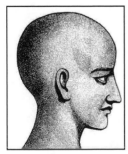

© 2002
The Critical Thinking Co.
(BRIGHT MINDS ™)
www.criticalthinking.com
P.O. Box 1610 • Seaside • CA 93955
Phone 800-458-4849 • FAX 831-393-3277
ISBN 978-0-89455-810-8

About Dr. Funster's Think-A-Minutes

This collection of fast, fun riddles, puzzles, and teasers develops thinking skills for higher grades and top test scores. The activities are perfect for school, home, and travel. They are very popular as brain start, extra credit, sponge, or reward activities.

This collection is taken from a variety of past and current books published by Critical Thinking Books & Software. If you would like to see more of a particular type of activity, refer to page 45 for other pages with similar activities in this book or for the names of the series from which the activities were taken.

For other books with similar activities, call 800-458-4849 for the store nearest you or to order directly.

Dressing Logic

DIRECTIONS: Agnes, Barbara, Catherine, and Diana are going to a party. Below are the true statements they made about what they would wear. Decide what blouses they wear to the party, based on the illustration at the bottom of the page.

Agnes: "I will wear 👟👟 and/or   ."

Barbara: "I will wear 👟👟 and/or   ."

Catherine: "I will wear 👟👟 and/or   ."

Diana: "I will wear 👟👟 and/or   ."

Based on the shoes the girls chose to wear, which blouse(s) could each girl wear and still make the statement true? (The girls always tell the truth.)

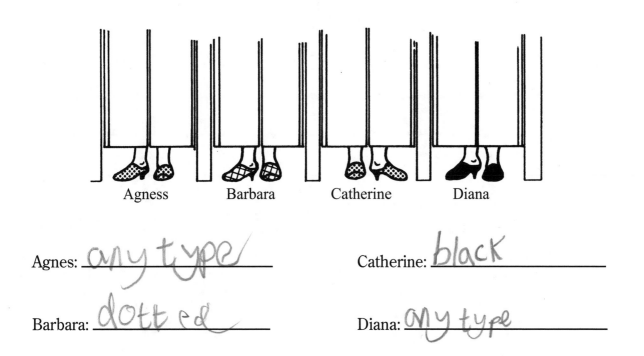

Agnes: _any type_   Catherine: _black_

Barbara: _dotted_   Diana: _any type_

Think Twice

1. A doctor gives a man eight pills and tells him to take one every three hours, starting now. If the man does as he is told, how long will it be until he has taken all of the pills?

2. A cyclone fence needs a fence post every three meters. Mrs. Brown's yard is 21 meters wide. How many fence posts will this yard need for its width?

Hiding in Plain View

1. How many triangles do you see?

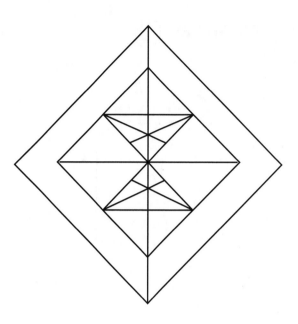

2. How many squares do you see?

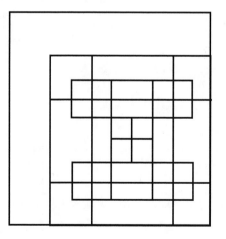

Be a "Gram" Cracker

DIRECTIONS: Interpret the verbal puzzles and write a common phrase for each in the blanks.

EXAMPLE:

K
C
A
R
C

means "crack up" since it is "crack" written upwards!

1.

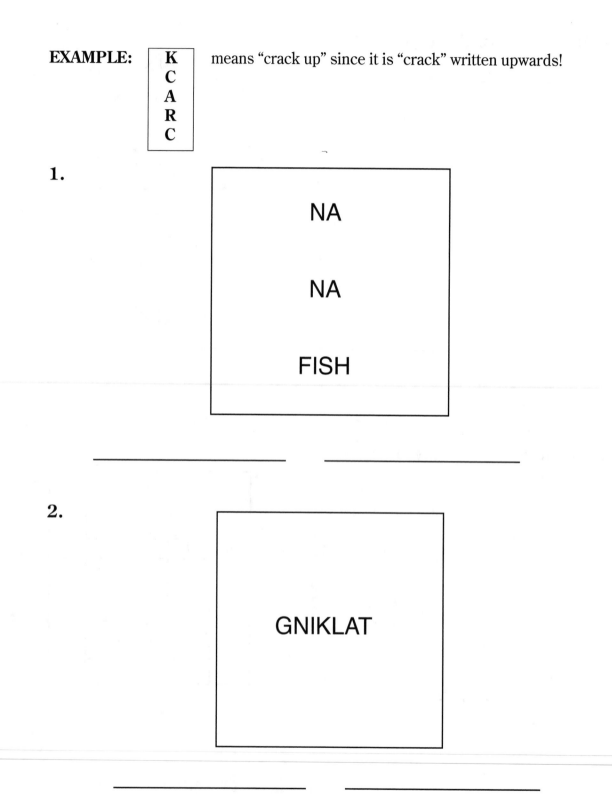

NA

NA

FISH

_____   _____

2.

GNIKLAT

_____   _____

From *Think-A-Grams Book B1*. For more activities like the ones above, call 800-458-4849 for the store nearest you or to order directly. © 2002 The Critical Thinking Co. • www.criticalthinking.com

SquArea

DIRECTIONS: Find the areas of the following figures. Draw in the parts as you see them. The dots are spaced 1/4 inch apart. Fill in the answer sentences.

EXAMPLE:

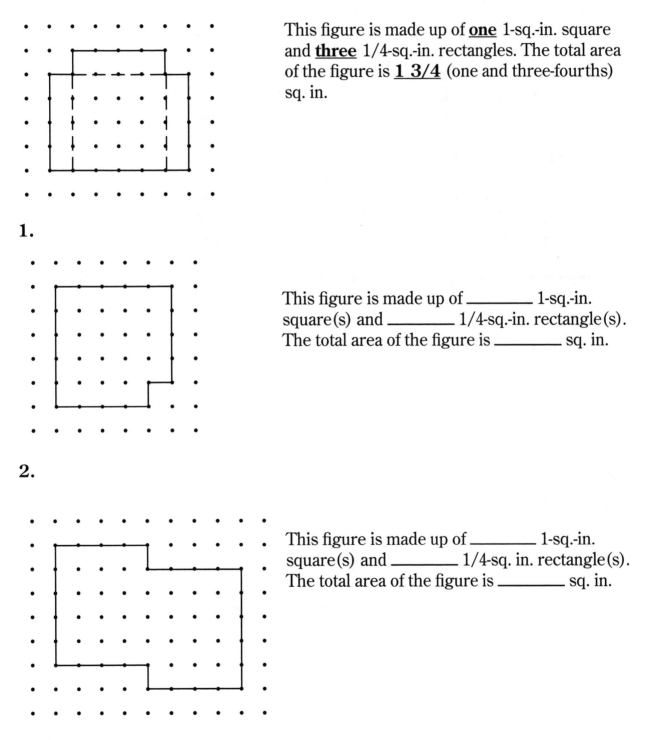

This figure is made up of **one** 1-sq.-in. square and **three** 1/4-sq.-in. rectangles. The total area of the figure is **1 3/4** (one and three-fourths) sq. in.

1.

This figure is made up of _____ 1-sq.-in. square(s) and _____ 1/4-sq.-in. rectangle(s). The total area of the figure is _____ sq. in.

2.

This figure is made up of _____ 1-sq.-in. square(s) and _____ 1/4-sq. in. rectangle(s). The total area of the figure is _____ sq. in.

The Trouble Maker

Rocky was always getting into trouble. It was nearly always his fault. He seemed to go with trouble the way syrup goes with pancakes. One day Rocky came into class after lunch, and he had a black eye. The teacher asked what happened, and Rocky said he ran into a door. Chuck knew that Big Mike, an older boy, had been picking on Rocky all week and had finally cornered Rocky this noon. When Rocky had started to walk away, Big Mike had given him the black eye.

The teacher didn't know this, but he knew Rocky well enough to know that Rocky didn't get the black eye by walking into any door. So the teacher said, "Rocky, I don't believe you. I know the way you're always starting trouble. I think you've been fighting again. I'm sending you to the principal's office." Rocky started for the door.

Chuck didn't know whether or not to tell the teacher what had really happened. Chuck knew that if Rocky didn't tell the teacher, then he wouldn't tell the principal, either. So it looked as though if Chuck didn't tell the teacher what happened, then Rocky would get into trouble both with the teacher and with the principal. But if Chuck did tell what happened, then maybe Rocky would be mad at him. After all, there was nothing to keep Rocky from telling what really happened, was there? And it wasn't really Chuck's business, anyhow, was it?

If you were Chuck, what would you do?

What do you think Chuck should do?

Cross-Section Logic

DIRECTIONS: Use the illustrations below to decide if each statement is always true. Write YES or NO in each blank.

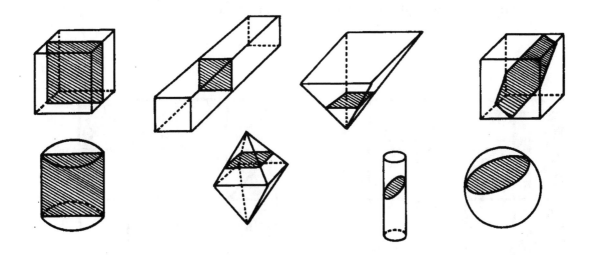

1. If it is a cube, then it has a cross section that is a square. _____

2. If it is not a cube, then it does not have a cross section that is a square.

_____

3. If it has a cross section that is a square, then it is a cube. _____

4. If it does not have a cross section that is a square, then it is not a cube.

_____

Have "Sum" Fun

DIRECTIONS: Fill in the white squares using the following rules:
- A number below a diagonal line shows the sum for the squares underneath.
- A number above a diagonal line shows the sum for the squares to the right.
- You may use only the digits 1 through 9 (one digit per square).
- You may not use any digit more than once to get a sum.

1.

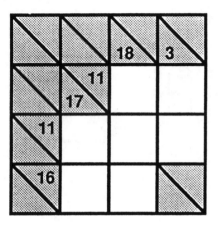

2.

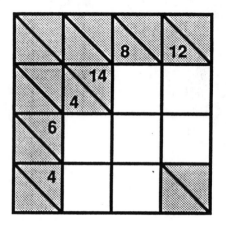

3.

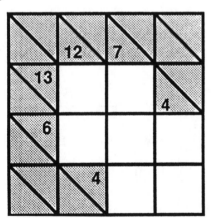

4.

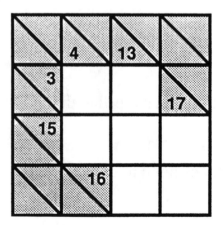

Matrix Fill-Up

DIRECTIONS: In this exercise, each column must contain words belonging to the class represented by the column heading. The words in each row should begin with the letter in the first column. Some of the boxes are filled in to help you get started.

FIRST LETTER	BEVERAGE	BUILDING	ENTERTAIN-MENT	FOOD
C	Coffee	Cabin	Circus	Cheese
G			Golf	
M		Museum		
S	Soda			
T				Toast

Riddle Time

DIRECTIONS: The answer to each riddle may be a word or part of a word.

1.
> With mist I'm a wrong,
> That says you need some drilling;
> With tooth a problem,
> A hole in need of filling.
>
> *What am I?* _____

2.
> I am just a part,
> Somewhat less than a whole;
> Or think of war's end,
> No soldier's funeral.
>
> *What am I?* _____

3.
> My coo is a drink,
> Refreshing in heat;
> An egg must be me,
> Or no one will eat.
>
> *What am I?* _____

4.
> With t I'm the crime,
> Of country betrayed;
> Alone I'm the grounds,
> In argument made.
>
> *What am I?* _____

Land Plots

DIRECTIONS: On the following map, the space between two adjacent dots = one mile. Finish drawing the map as described below.

1. Point ○ is a corner of Mr. Perez's property. His land extends four miles south and three miles west of point ○. Draw a diagram of Mr. Perez's land.

2. Point ○ is also a corner of Ms. Vukovich's property. Her land extends three miles east and two miles south of point ○. Draw a diagram of Ms. Vukovich's land.

3. How much of Mr. Perez's land touches Ms. Vukovich's land?

Catch A Code

DIRECTIONS: Figure out what letter each picture represents. Match each letter to its corresponding picture to figure out the 7 math words below. (Hint: Trophy = T.)

SUITCASE = O   STAR = e   PRESENT = V

PHONE = L   LEAF = I   BALL = ∩

CAR = D   CAT = M   TROPHY = T

TREE = S   HORSESHOE = K   COMPUTER = h

Analogy Alley

Mia
Mia

DIRECTIONS: Circle the best word to complete each analogy. (Hint: Some word choices could be used as a noun or a verb.)

1. cartilage : shark :: bone : _____

    rigid
    chicken
    arm
    skeleton

2. waterfall : cascade :: stream : _____

    water
    puddle
    ocean
    river

3. runner : jog :: bicyclist : _____

    pedal
    leg
    bicycle
    race

4. flu : virus :: infection : _____

    illness
    cut
    cold
    bacteria

5. latitude : longitude :: horizontal : _____

    globe
    vertical
    line
    direction

6. senator : legislature :: judge : _____

    client
    law
    criminal
    judiciary

7. mansion : wealth :: shack : _____

    poverty
    hut
    shame
    money

A Fresh Look

1. **a.** At a store display, identical cubes are stacked in the corner as shown. How many of the cubes are not visible?

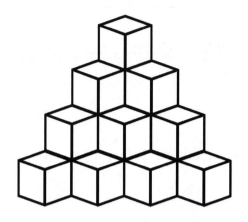

   b. Suppose there were an additional layer with 5 blocks visible on the bottom. Then how many of the cubes would not be visible?

2. What angle do the hands of a clock really make at 3:30?

Go Figure

DIRECTIONS: For every figure in the left column, there is a figure at the right with the same area. Draw a line between each pair of shapes having the same area.

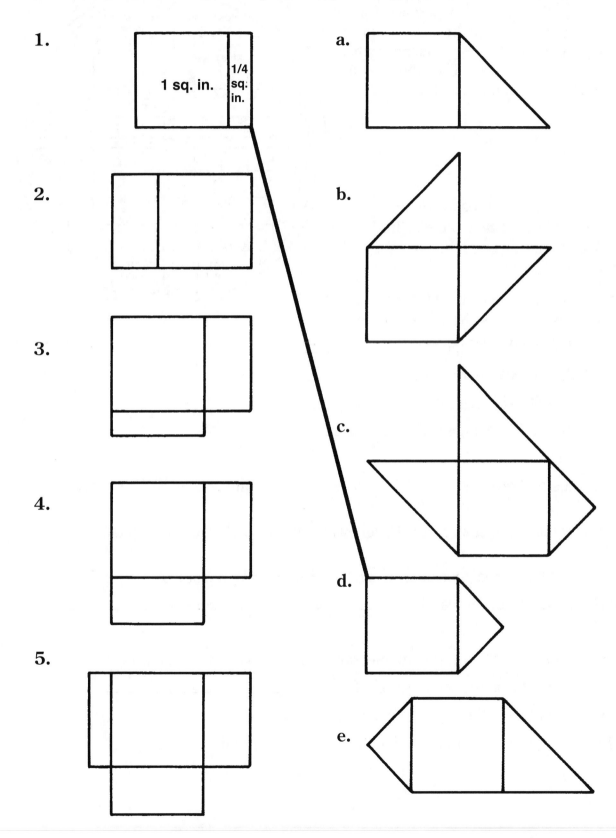

Where Is It?

DIRECTIONS: Some cities are divided into four sections: northwest, northeast, southwest, and southeast. In this example the east-west streets are identified by numbers and the north-south streets by letters. For example, A Street in the northeast section is called A St. NE. The other sections contain A St. NW, A St. SW, and A St. SE.

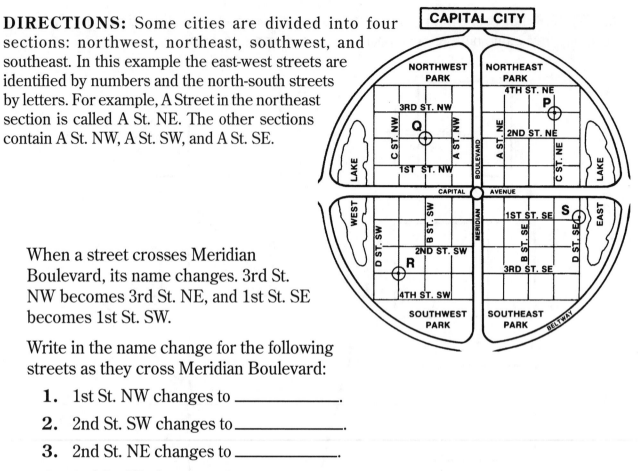

When a street crosses Meridian Boulevard, its name changes. 3rd St. NW becomes 3rd St. NE, and 1st St. SE becomes 1st St. SW.

Write in the name change for the following streets as they cross Meridian Boulevard:

1. 1st St. NW changes to _____.

2. 2nd St. SW changes to _____.

3. 2nd St. NE changes to _____.

4. 3rd St. SE changes to _____.

When a street crosses Capital Avenue, its name changes. B St. SW becomes B St. NW, and A St. NE becomes A St. SE.

Write in the name change for the following streets as they cross Capital Avenue:

5. D. St. SW becomes _____. **7.** A St. NW becomes _____.

6. C St. NW becomes _____. **8.** B St. SE becomes _____.

EXAMPLE: Point P is at the intersection of 3rd St. NE and C St. NE.

9. Point Q is at the intersection of _____ and _____.

10. Point R is at the intersection of _____ and _____.

11. Point S is at the intersection of _____ and _____.

Think 'em and Link 'em!

DIRECTIONS: A think 'em link 'em is a pair of two-syllable rhyming words that is defined by a given phrase. To form a think 'em link 'em, study the clue phrase and think of two rhyming words that are synonyms for the key words in the phrase; for example, a fake horse is a "phony pony." Can you think of two words that have a meaning similar to *a heavier slugger*? The think 'em link 'em would be a "fatter batter." Draw a line from the phrase on the left to its think 'em link 'em on the right.

Phrase	**Think 'em link 'em**
1. beach sweets	wider spider
2. an accumulating tenant	fable label
3. a chocolate-candy fight	faker baker
4. a tin flower part	chipper skipper
5. an odd game warden	hoarder boarder
6. a pretend chef	stranger ranger
7. a fatter arachnid	tender fender
8. a story tag	metal petal
9. a happy captain	sandy candy
10. a sensitive bumper	truffle scuffle

Move It!

1. The football goal post shows a ball going through the uprights. Move exactly two parts of the goal post so the ball is no longer between the uprights but there is still a goal post.

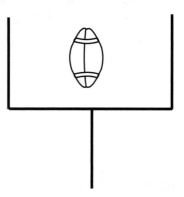

Explain how you got your answer.

_____

_____

_____

2. Six circles are arranged in an "L" shape with the horizontal part containing 3 circles and the vertical part containing 4 circles. The corner circle is counted as both horizontal and vertical. Move one circle so there are 4 circles in both the horizontal and vertical parts of the "L."

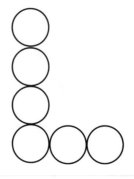

The Hasty Letter

Mary was very angry at Bart. She wrote him a letter telling him what a rat he was, and she mailed it the same day. The next day she found out that someone had lied to her about Bart, and she should not have been angry at Bart. She was sorry she had mailed the letter, but she didn't know what to do about it.

She couldn't hide around Bart's house until the mail was delivered and then take her letter back, because that would be breaking the law. But she couldn't let Bart read the letter either, because she had written some pretty strong things to him in the letter, and she was sorry now.

If you were Mary, what would you do?

What do you think Mary should do?

Riddle Time

DIRECTIONS: The answer to each riddle may be a word or part of a word.

1.
> Alone I am words
> Entering your mind;
> With fur I am slaves,
> Leaving chains behind.
>
> *What am I?* _____

2.
> With trick I am power,
> On which we do depend;
> Alone I am to choose,
> Who will win in the end.
>
> *What am I?* _____

3.
> They cooked all of my kin,
> But I felt no rancor;
> Or think of a harbor,
> Where boats can drop anchor.
>
> *What am I?* _____

4.
> With ul I'm the one,
> Who gets the army moving;
> With us I'm the sense,
> Of giving and approving.
>
> *What am I?* _____

It Takes Five

DIRECTIONS: Use five 2s to make each number listed below. Rules of order apply (e.g., make 506 using five 2s: $22^2 + 22 = 506$).

1. _____ = 3

2. _____ = 18

3. _____ = 119

4. _____ = 42

5. _____ = 34

6. _____ = 26

7. _____ = 12

8. _____ = 30

The Game Reserve

DIRECTIONS: Use the clues to enter the correct digits. In the clues, "A" means *across* and "D" means *down*. For example, "1-D" would refer to clue number 1 DOWN. Each square takes a single digit from 0 through 9. No answer begins with 0.

A zebra, an elephant, and a giraffe met for lunch yesterday in Kenya's Masai Mara Game Reserve where Mr. Suhali is a game warden.

The animals found that the giraffe was twice as old as the elephant, that the zebra's age was halfway between the elephant's and the giraffe's, and that the age of the elephant's Great-Aunt Martha was 10 years more than the sum of the other three ages.

ACROSS

1. Elephant's age

2. Giraffe's age

4. Sum of digits of 1-D

6. Other zebras in zebra's herd

7. 23 x 10-A

9. Trees Great-Aunt Martha uprooted last week

10. Sum of 2-A and 3-D

DOWN

1. 10 more than product of 6-A and 7-A

2. Years Mr. Suhali has been at Masai Mara Game Reserve

3. 10 less than Great-Aunt Martha's age

5. Age of Mr. Suhali's father

8. Age of Mr. Suhali's Great-Uncle Mortimer

11. Zebra's age

From *Math Mind Benders® Book A1.* For more activities like the one above, call 800-458-4849 for the store nearest you or to order directly. © 2002 The Critical Thinking Co. • www.criticalthinking.com

Describe in Writing

DIRECTIONS: In the blanks below, write a description of the hairstyle. Refer only to the picture on this page, and write in complete sentences. Details are important!
Separate the picture from the finished description and pass the description to someone else. Have him or her locate and circle the picture on the next page, using only your description. If s/he is getting frustrated, change your description so it can be used to find the picture.

My Description

_____

_____

_____

_____

_____

_____

Describe in Writing, continued

When Were They Born?

DIRECTIONS: Two boys and two girls (Alexander, Bertha, Glenn, Hiroko), whose last names are Kraft, Loring, Silverman, and Tyndall, were born in different months (January, February, May, October) of the same year. Find out their names and birth months. Use the chart to help you. (Put "X" on squares showing what is NOT true and put checks on squares showing what IS true.)

1. Glenn was born after Tyndall and before Hiroko.

2. Bertha is older than Kraft and younger than Loring.

3. Silverman is not the youngest, and Tyndall is not the oldest.

	Kraft	Loring	Silverman	Tyndall	January	February	May	October
Alexander								
Bertha								
Glenn								
Hiroko								
January				
February				
May				
October				

Bending Words

DIRECTIONS: Complete the word series. Each word in the series is like the one before it in many ways and different from it in some ways. The circles indicate letters to be changed. The Definition Box gives the meanings of the words in the series. The Definition Box can be used, if needed, for clues and should be used to check your answers.

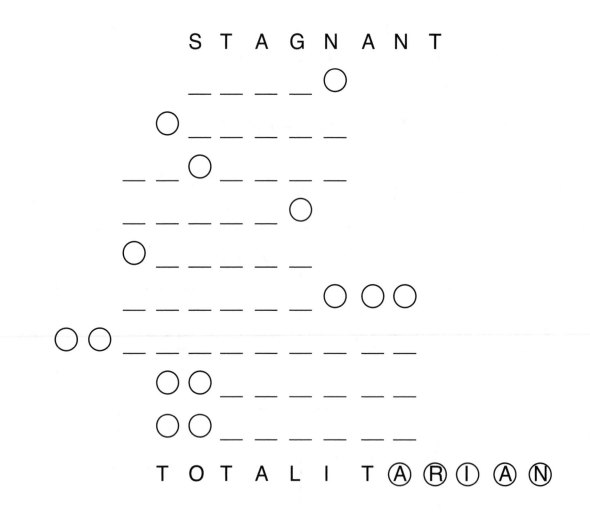

S T A G N A N T

_ _ _ _ ◯

◯ _ _ _ _ _

_ _ ◯ _ _ _ _

_ _ _ _ ◯ _

◯ _ _ _ _ _

_ _ _ _ _ ◯ ◯ ◯

◯◯ _ _ _ _ _ _ _ _ _

◯◯ _ _ _ _ _ _

◯◯ _ _ _ _ _ _

T O T A L I T ⒜ ⓡ ⓘ ⒜ ⓝ

Definition Box

an aggregate	death rate	disastrous death
entryway	human	lasting fame
one-party government	raised platform	stamps
standing still	transporting boats	

Think Quick!

1. When 1/3 of the year is left, what month comes next?

2. What numbers go in the corner boxes to make the sum along each of the three lines 27? Use numbers 6–11, each only once.

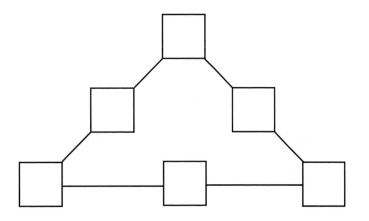

3. How many even numbers between 300 and 400 have a 3 in them?

PARTNER/GROUP
ACTIVITY

How's Your "Herring"?

DIRECTIONS: The statement below is misleading—things are not as they first appear! The statement refers to an event based on a science concept. Ask yes-or-no questions of your teacher (or someone who knows the answer) to get clues. Use as few questions as possible to figure out and describe the situation. Make every question count!

Example: Out for a drive, he stopped for gas, but when he filled up, the fuel indicator never budged. Why not?

Answer: He was filling the tires of his car with air. Science concept: A gas is not a liquid or a solid. Gases, liquids, and solids are differentiated by their properties. In a gas, atoms do not stick together; a gas is compressible. The atoms of a liquid or solid do stick together and the substance is not compressible.)

The police shot at him as he made his getaway, but he never even slowed down. They didn't bother pursuing him. Why not?

Simple Complications

1. A certain kind of bacteria doubles in quantity every hour. At midnight two nights ago, only two of these bacteria were in a jar. At midnight last night, the jar was full. At what time was the jar half full?

2. Is the following statement true, or is it false?

THIS STATEMENT IS FALSE.

Box Logic

DIRECTIONS: Figures are hidden in boxes 1, 2, 3, and 4. Using the rules on each box, determine which figures can be hidden where.

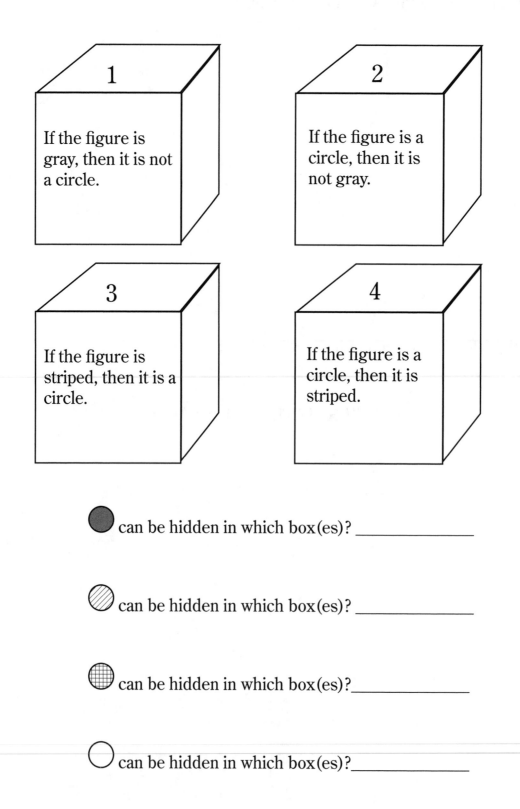

1

If the figure is gray, then it is not a circle.

2

If the figure is a circle, then it is not gray.

3

If the figure is striped, then it is a circle.

4

If the figure is a circle, then it is striped.

⬤ can be hidden in which box(es)? _____

◯ (striped) can be hidden in which box(es)? _____

◯ (grid) can be hidden in which box(es)? _____

◯ can be hidden in which box(es)? _____

Be a "Gram" Cracker

DIRECTIONS: Interpret the verbal puzzles and write each, as a common phrase, in the blanks.

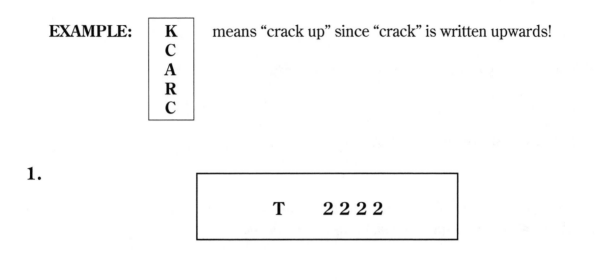

EXAMPLE:

| K |
| C |
| A |
| R |
| C |

means "crack up" since "crack" is written upwards!

1.

T   2 2 2 2

_____ _____ _____

2.

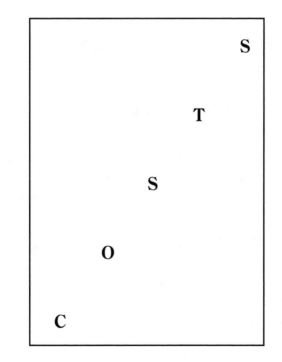

_____ _____

A Question of Relevance

DIRECTIONS: Mario wants to be either a firefighter or a plumber, but he can't decide which he wants to be. He is talking about it with his friend John. John is trying to help him make up his mind. Which of John's statements sound like they are relevant to Mario's problem? Circle their numbers.

1. Firefighting is more dangerous than plumbing.

2. I have a cousin who is a firefighter.

3. I have a cousin who is a firefighter and another who is a plumber. You could talk to them and hear what they say about their jobs.

4. Firefighters work around the clock. You couldn't always plan to go some place at night, because you might have to work then.

5. You might not like firefighting.

6. You're not strong enough to be a firefighter.

7. Plumbers make more money than firefighters.

8. There's a shortage both of good plumbers and of good firefighters.

In the Pink with Red Herrings

DIRECTIONS: The statement below is misleading—things are not as they first appear! The statement refers to an event based on a science concept. Ask yes-or-no questions of your teacher (or someone who knows the answer) to get clues. Use as few questions as possible to figure out and describe the situation. Make every question count!

   Example: Out for a drive, he stopped for gas, but when he filled up, the fuel indicator never budged. Why not?

   Answer: He was filling the tires of his car with air. Science concept: A gas is not a liquid or a solid. Gases, liquids, and solids are differentiated by their properties. In a gas, atoms do not stick together; a gas is compressible. The atoms of a liquid or solid do stick together and the substance is not compressible.)

When the class needed his help, Phil resisted. The teacher put Phil at the head of the class. Why? Who or what was Phil?

Look Again

DIRECTIONS: In each exercise, give the next figure in the series.

1.

Ɯ T M T Ⱶ S ? ___

2. These are different views of a solid object. Draw either side view.

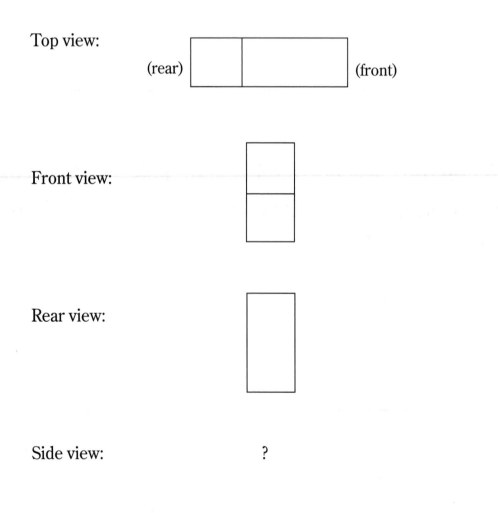

Top view: (rear) [   ] (front)

Front view:

Rear view:

Side view: ?

Regnads

DIRECTIONS: Look at the objects in the set called Regnads. What attributes do they have in common that makes them members of this set? On another sheet of paper, describe these attributes so that someone reading your description could name or draw a member of the same set. Keep in mind that there may be more Regnads than just the ones you see below. When you are finished, give the description to a partner, who will then name or draw a member of the set called "Regnads."

FLAMMABLE
This is a Regnad.

FIRST AID
This is not a Regnad.

NO SMOKING
This is not a Regnad.

POISON
This is a Regnad.

SLIPPERY FLOOR
This is a Regnad.

FIRE EXTINGUISHER
This is not a Regnad.

_____

_____

_____

_____

_____

_____

From *Critical Thinking Activities to Improve Writing Skills: Whatcha-Macallits
Book A1*. For more activities like the one above, call 800-458-4849 for the store nearest
you or to order directly. © 2002 The Critical Thinking Co. • www.criticalthinking.com

The Census Taker

DIRECTIONS: A census taker stopped at a lady's house and wanted to find out how many children she had. The lady, a math teacher, wanted to see if the census taker still knew his math. Read their conversation and explain how the census taker figured out the ages. Don't quit! Start by trying some numbers.

Census taker to lady: How many children do you have?

Lady: Three.

Census taker: How old are they?

Lady: The product of their ages is 36.

Census taker: That's not enough information.

Lady: The sum of their ages is our house number.

Census taker (looking at the house number): Still not enough information.

Lady: My oldest child plays the piano.

Census taker: Aha! I know now. Thank you!

The three ages: _____   _____   _____

From *Math Ties Book B1*. For more activities like the one above, call 800-458-4849 for the store nearest you or to order directly. © 2002 The Critical Thinking Co. • www.criticalthinking.com

Be a "Gram" Cracker

DIRECTIONS: Interpret the verbal puzzles and write each, as a common phrase, in the blanks.

EXAMPLE:

means "crack up" since "crack" is written upwards!

1.

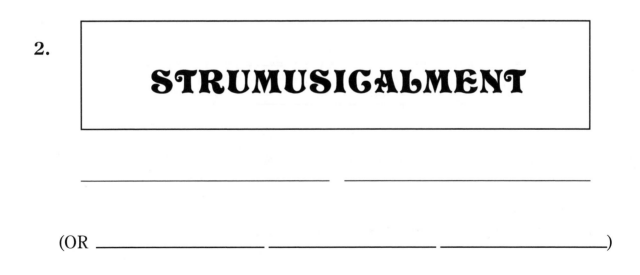

_____   _____   _____   _____

2.

STRUMUSICALMENT

_____   _____

(OR _____   _____   _____)

Finding Relationships

DIRECTIONS: For each line of the chart, read the first two words and decide how they are related. Then read the third word and think of a word to write in the last box. The last two words should be related in the same way as the first two words. Possible answers are given upside-down in scrambled order at the bottom of the page.

amateur	professional	school band	
cheap	expensive	burlap	
fast	slow	greased lightning	
pleasure	pain	compliment	
up	down	raise	

insult, lower, molasses in January, New York Philharmonic, silk

From *Basic Thinking Skills: Analogies–B.* For more activities like the one above, call 800-458-4849 for the store nearest you or to order directly. © 2002 The Critical Thinking Co. • www.criticalthinking.com

From Start to Finish

DIRECTIONS: Describe what was done to the starting figure to make it end up like the finished figure. There may be more than one answer. (Note that the numbers have been kept in their original orientation for ease of reading.)

EXAMPLE:

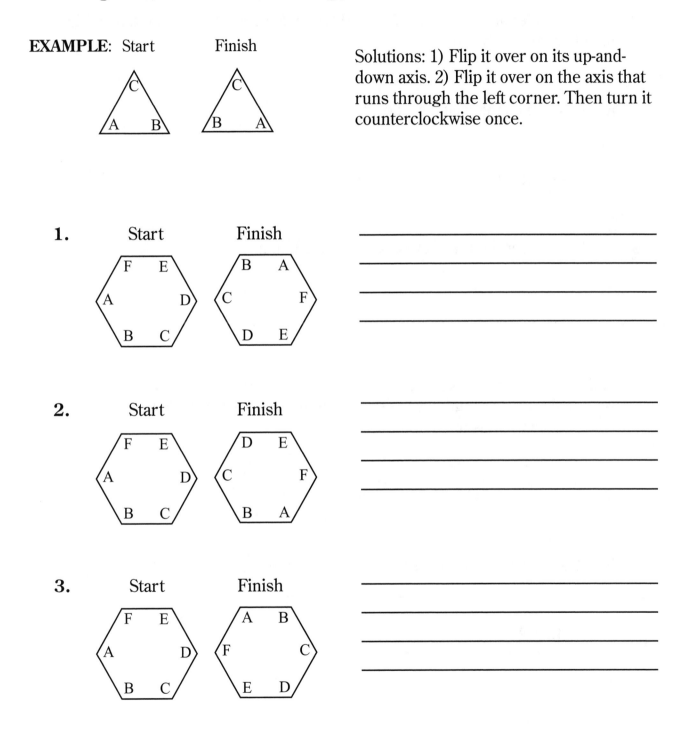

Solutions: 1) Flip it over on its up-and-down axis. 2) Flip it over on the axis that runs through the left corner. Then turn it counterclockwise once.

Test Your Logic

DIRECTIONS: Circle the correct answer (a, b, or c) for each logic problem.

1. Anna is louder and older than Rita and Linda. Nate is louder than Rita and Linda but older than only Linda.

    a. It is certain that Nate is older than Anna.

    b. It is certain that Nate is younger than Anna.

    c. It is not certain that Nate is louder than Linda.

2. Some brilliant students do not need to do homework to receive good grades in school. All average students need to do homework to receive better grades in school. Larry needs to do homework.

    a. It is certain that Larry is an average student.

    b. It is certain that Larry is not a brilliant student.

    c. Neither A nor B.

From *Revenge of the Logic Spiders* software. For more activities like the ones above, call 800-458-4849 for the store nearest you or to order directly. © 2002 The Critical Thinking Co. • www.criticalthinking.com

ANSWER KEY

Page 1: Dressing Logic

Agnes: any type
Barbara: dotted
Catherine: black
Diana: any type

Page 2: Think Twice

1. 21 hours (he takes one right away, so you add 3 x 7, not 3 x 8)
2. 8 (start with one post then add 21 ÷ 3; 1 + 7 = 8)

Page 3: Hiding in Plain View

52 triangles
42 squares

Page 4: Be a "Gram" Cracker

tuna fish
talking back

Page 5: SquArea

1. one, two, 1 2/4 or 1 1/2
2. two, two, 2 2/4 or 2 1/2

Page 6: The Trouble Maker

(answers vary)

Page 7: Cross-Section Logic

1. NO, 2. NO, 3. NO, 4. NO

Page 8: Have "Sum" Fun

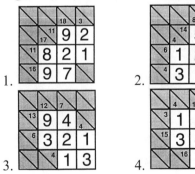

Page 9: Matrix Fill-Up

Answers may vary. Here are some examples:

FIRST LETTER	BEVERAGE	BUILDING	ENTERTAIN-MENT	FOOD
C	Coffee	Cabin	Circus	Cheese
G	Grapejuice	Garage	Golf	Grapefruit
M	Milk	Museum	Movie	Meat
S	Soda	School	Sports	Steak
T	Tea	Theater	Television	Toast

Page 10: Riddle Time

1. mistake, toothache
2. piece, peace
3. Kool-aid®, laid
4. treason, reason

Page 11: Land Plots

1, 2:

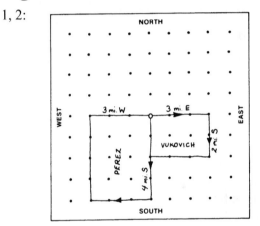

3. two miles

Page 12: Catch a Code

Suitcase = O
Phone = L
Car = D
Tree = S
Star = E
Leaf = I
Cat = M
Horseshoe = A
Present = V
Ball = N
Trophy = T
Computer = H

1. One
2. Total
3. Add
4. Math
5. Seven
6. Nine
7. Ten

Page 13: Analogy Alley

1. chicken (part of)
2. river (synonym)
3. pedal (object-action)
4. bacteria (product of)
5. vertical (antonym)
6. judiciary (someone who)
7. poverty (association)

Page 14: A Fresh Look

1. a. There are 10 cubes not visible.
   b. With a bottom visible row of 5, the answer is 20 cubes not visible.
2. The clock hands make an angle of 75 degrees (not 90, since the little hand is between 3 and 4). There is 12 1/2 minutes difference between the hands.

Page 15: Go Figure

1. d (given)
2. a
3. e
4. b
5. c

Page 16: Where Is It?

1. 1st Street NE
2. 2nd Street SE
3. 2nd Street NW
4. 3rd Street SW
5. D Street NW
6. C Street SW
7. A Street SW
8. B Street NE
9. 2nd Street NW and B Street NW
10. 3rd Street SW and C Street SW
11. 1st Street SE and D Street SE

Page 17: Think 'em and Link 'em!

1. sandy candy
2. hoarder boarder
3. truffle scuffle
4. metal petal
5. stranger ranger
6. faker baker
7. wider spider
8. fable label
9. chipper skipper
10. tender fender

Page 18: Move It!

1. The new goal post is upside down. Slide the horizontal bar right so that the left end is over the base of the goal post. Put the left upright at the right end of the horizontal bar and move it down to the ground. (See illustration.)

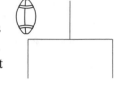

2. Move the top circle from the vertical part so it is on top of the corner circle (bird's-eye view).

Page 19: The Hasty Letter

Answers will vary.

Page 20: Riddle Time

1. read, freed
2. electric, elect
3. bacon, bay
4. general, generous

Page 21: It Takes Five

1. $2 \div 2 + 2 + 2 - 2 = 3$
2. $(2 + 2)(2 + 2) + 2 = 18$
3. $(22 \div 2)^2 - 2 = 119$
4. $2(22 - 2) + 2 = 42$
5. $(2 + 2 + 2)^2 - 2 = 34$
6. $(2 + 2)^2 + 22 = 26$
7. $2 \div 2 + 22 \div 2 = 12$
8. $2(2 + 2)^2 - 2 = 30$

Page 22: The Game Reserve

¹6	²1	³2
⁴2 ⁵5		⁶7
⁷8 9	⁸7	
⁹9	¹⁰3	¹¹9

2-A must be an even number and so is at least 12, making 1-A at least 6. Then the answers for 1-A, 2-A, 11-D, and 3-D are respectively, 6, 12, 9, and 27. (Any higher number for 1-A does not result in a one-digit answer for 11-D.) Answers are now forced for 2-D, 6-A, 10-A, 7-A, 8-D, 1-D, 9-A, 4-A, and 5-D.

Page 23–24: Describe in Writing

Possible descriptions for hairstyle:
Style: moussed spikes, straight hair
Length: short
Color: dark
Hairline: down and rounded on forehead
Direction combed: back on sides; straight up on top
Decoration: none

Page 25: When Were They Born?

The person born in October is not Loring (2), Silverman (3), or Tyndall (1), so he or she is Kraft. Tyndall, not born in May (1) or January (3), was born in February. Loring, not born in May (2), was born in January. Then Silverman was born in May.

Loring, born in January, is not Glenn or Hiroko (1) or Bertha (2), so Loring is Alexander. Tyndall is not Glenn or Hiroko (1), so Tyndall is Bertha. Kraft, born in October, is not Glenn (1), so Kraft is Hiroko, and then Silverman is Glenn.

FIRST NAME	LAST NAME	MONTH
Alexander	Loring	January
Bertha	Tyndall	February
Glenn	Silverman	May
Hiroko	Kraft	October

Page 26: Bending Words

STAGNANT (standing still)
STAGE (raised platform)
POSTAGE (stamps)
PORTAGE (transporting boats)
PORTAL (entryway)
MORTAL (human)
MORTALITY (death rate)
IMMORTALITY (lasting fame)
FATALITY (disastrous death)
TOTALITY (an aggregate)
TOTALITARIAN (one-party government)

Page 27: Think Quick!

1. September. Since 2/3 of 12 is 8, the 8th month is over and the 9th is beginning.
2. 11, 10, 9. The three sums are 11 + 6 + 10, 11 + 7 + 9, and 9 + 8 + 10.
3. 50. There are 100 numbers, all beginning with 3. Half of those are even.

Page 28: How's Your "Herring"?

1. The police shot at him as he made his getaway, but he never even slowed down. They didn't bother pursuing him. Why not?
   Answer: He was "shot" with a radar gun to see how fast he was going. Since he wasn't speeding, the police allowed him to continue on his vacation "getaway."
   Concept: Microwaves reflect off objects; they can be used to determine the speed of an object. The waves are directed at the moving object, and the frequency of the "bounced" return waves is measured.

Page 29: Simple Complications

1. 11:00 p.m. last night.
2. Neither. The statement cannot be true, for if it were, then it would be false by its own admission and thus would be both true and false at the same time. On the other hand, it cannot be false, for it it were false, then it would be stating the truth and so would be both false and true at the same time.

Page 30: Box Logic

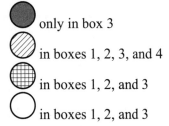

only in box 3
in boxes 1, 2, 3, and 4
in boxes 1, 2, and 3
in boxes 1, 2, and 3

Page 31: Be a "Gram" Cracker

1. tea for two (T and 4 twos)
2. rising costs

Page 32: A Question of Relevance

1. Yes
2. No
3. Yes
4. Yes
5. No (He might not like any job, but a person usually doesn't know whether or not he likes it until after he's done it a while.)
6. Yes
7. Yes
8. No (We've already said Mike wants to be in one of the two occupations. This might be a relevant statement if John were trying to talk him into being a firefighter or a plumber instead of something else, but it is not relevant under the conditions stated.)

Page 33: In the Pink with Red Herrings

1. The teacher wanted to show a diagram at the front of the classroom, but it was too dark to see. Phil was a filament (coiled tungsten wire) in an incandescent light bulb. When the teacher switched on the light, the filament resisted the electric current. As a result, the wire heated up and gave off light.
   Concept: Electric energy is transmitted through a conducting material. Most conductors offer some resistance to the current. Electric current passing through resistance creates heat—an often undesirable effect. In electric heaters and incandescent light bulbs, however, resistance is desired because it results in heat and light.

Page 34: Look Again

1. S (the pattern is made up of the first letters of the days of the week; every other one is upside down)
2.

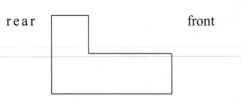

Page 35: Regnads

A **Regnad** is a sign that warns of danger. (Smoking is hazardous to your health but a "no smoking" sign just indicates smoking is not allowed in this area.) Clue: take a backwards look at regnad!

Page 36: The Census Taker

List all the possibilities for 3 factors of 36:		Sum of their ages is house number	
6 x 6 x 1 =	36	6 + 6 + 1 =	13
4 x 9 x 1 =	36	4 + 9 + 1 =	14
2 x 18 x 1 =	36	2 + 18 + 1 =	21
3 x 12 x 1 =	36	3 + 12 + 1 =	16
6 x 2 x 3 =	36	6 + 2 + 3 =	11
4 x 3 x 3 =	36	4 + 3 + 3 =	10
2 x 9 x 2 =	36	2 + 9 + 2 =	13

Notice that two sets have sums of 13, which is why the census taker could not yet determine the answer. As soon as the lady said that the *oldest* child plays the piano, he knew the ages must be 2, 9, and 2 (the combination that has an eldest).

Page 37: Be a "Gram" Cracker

1. no swimming after dark
2. musical instrument (*musical* in *strument*)

Page 38: Finding Relationships

New York Philharmonic, silk, molasses in January, insult, lower

Page 39: From Start to Finish

Possible answers:
1. Turn twice clockwise.
2. Turn twice counter clockwise then flip along axis that goes through lower right vertex.
3. Turn twice clockwise then flip along axis that goes through upper left vertex.

Page 40: Test Your Logic

1. b (If Anna is older than Rita and Linda, but Nate is older than only Linda, then we can conclude that Nate is younger than Anna.)

2. c (Since only some brilliant students do not need to do homework, you cannot conclude what type of student Larry is.)

ACTIVITY/PRODUCT REFERENCE

PAGE NUMBER	ACTIVITY TITLE	SERIES TITLE	OTHER ACTIVITIES FROM THE SERIES
1	Dressing Logic	Visual Logic	p. 7, 30
2	Think Twice	Basic Thinking Skills	pp. 6, 19, 38
3	Hiding in Plain View	Brain Stretchers	pp. 12, 21, 34
4	Be a "Gram" Cracker	Think-A-Grams	pp. 31, 37
5	SquArea	Area Perception	p. 15
6	The Trouble Maker	Basic Thinking Skills	pp. 2, 19, 38
7	Cross-Section Logic	Visual Logic	p. 1, 30
8	Have "Sum" Fun	CrossNumber Puzzles	
9	Matrix Fill-Up	Verbal Classifications	
10	Riddle Time	Dr. DooRiddles	p. 20
11	Land Plots	Thinking Directionally	p. 16
12	Catch a Code	Brain Stretchers	pp. 3, 21, 34
13	Analogy Alley	Think Analogies	
14	A Fresh Look	Math Ties®	p. 36, 39
15	Go Figure	Area Perception	p. 5
16	Where Is It?	Thinking Directionally	p. 11
17	Think 'em and Link 'em!	Language Smarts	
18	Move It!	Scratch Your Brain	
19	The Hasty Letter	Basic Thinking Skills	pp. 2, 6, 38
20	Riddle Time	Dr. DooRiddles	p. 10
21	It Takes Five	Brain Stretchers	pp. 3, 12, 34
22	The Game Reserve	Math Mind Benders®	
23	Describe in Writing*	Critical Thinking Activities to Improve Writing Skills	p. 35
25	When Were They Born?	Mind Benders®	p. 22
26	Bending Words	Word Benders	
27	Think Quick!	Quick Thinks Math	
28	How's Your "Herring"?*	Red Herrings Science Mysteries	p. 33
29	Simple Complications	Classroom Quickies	
30	Box Logic	Visual Logic	p. 1, 7
31	Be a "Gram" Cracker	Think-A-Grams	p. 4, 37
32	A Question of Relevance	Inductive Thinking Skills	
33	In the Pink with Red Herrings*	Red Herrings Science Mysteries	p. 28
34	Look Again	Brain Stretchers	pp. 3, 12, 21
35	Regnads*	Critical Thinking Activities to Improve Writing Skills	p. 23
36	The Census Taker	Math Ties®	pp. 14, 39
37	Be a "Gram" Cracker	Think-A-Grams	p. 4, 31
38	Finding Relationships	Basic Thinking Skills	pp. 2, 6, 19
39	From Start to Finish	Math Ties®	pp. 14, 36
40	Test Your Logic	Revenge of the Logic Spiders software	

* Partner/Group Activity